MW00636194

Advent

PREPARING FOR CHRISTMAS

BY RON & LORI MOORE

© 2016 by Ron & Lori Moore. All rights reserved.

Published by Back to the Bible
6400 Cornhusker Highway
Lincoln, NE 68507
backtothebible.org

Written by Ronald D. and Lori J. Moore
Edited by Lori Moore and Heather Tyo
Cover and Interior Design by Kelly M. Vaughan

No part of this publication may be reproduced, stored in a retrieval system, or transmitted in any way by any means—electronic, mechanical, photocopy, recording, or otherwise—without the prior permission of the copyright holder, except as provided by USA copyright law.

The author has made every effort to trace the ownership of all quotes. In the event of a question arising from the use of a quote, we regret any error made and will be pleased to make the necessary correction in future editions of this book.

Unless otherwise indicated, all Scripture quotations are taken from the Holy Bible, New Living Translation, copyright ©1996, 2004, 2007, 2013, 2015 by Tyndale House Foundation. Used by permission of Tyndale House Publishers, Inc., Carol Stream, Illinois 60188. All rights reserved.

Scripture quotations marked (NIV) are taken from the Holy Bible, New International Version®, NIV®. Copyright © 1973, 1978, 1984, 2011 by Biblica, Inc.™ Used by permission of Zondervan (www.zondervan.com). All rights reserved worldwide. The "NIV" and "New International Version" are trademarks registered in the United States Patent and Trademark Office by Biblica, Inc.™

Table of Contents

HOW TO USE THIS GUIDE

✳ This guide begins with the first Sunday of Advent. The celebration order starts with Key Verse(s), followed by Lighting of the Candle(s), Christmas Carols, Passage to Read Aloud, Devotional, Closing Song, and Prayer.

✳ The first, second, and third Sunday celebrations are followed by six devotionals for the following week. These devotionals are purposed for personal reflection. You may want to read them individually, as a couple, or with your family. Since the calendar will vary regarding the number of days from the last Sunday until Christmas, we did not include devotionals following the fourth Sunday of Advent.

✳ Advent should be participatory. Involve your children. Have them read Scripture, light the candles, participate in a discussion, sing the carols, read a devotional, say the closing prayer, and blow out the candles. We have tried to keep the format simple, short, and to the point so your children will stay engaged.

✳ This is a great time to enjoy the Christmas carols. You can also sing some of the Christmas songs your children are already familiar with. The Christmas carols are taken from *Great Hymns of the Faith* (Zondervan). All of our children have noted that their favorite part of Advent has been singing the Christmas songs.

✳ At the end of this guide we have provided a journal for you to record special memories of Christmas. My wife, Lori, always dates her entries, which allows us to reflect on God's goodness, the events, and the fun we have had through the years.

A Note from the Authors

"Come over tonight and celebrate Advent with my family." My first thought to Lori's invitation was, "What in the world is Advent?" However, I was smitten. If she had invited me over to help cut the grass one blade at a time with scissors, I would have asked, "What time?"

When I arrived that evening to celebrate my first Advent, I followed her family into the living room. A wreath was on the table. There was a white candle in the middle of the wreath surrounded by four candles, one of which was pink. The Advent "service" included Scripture reading, prayer, the lighting of a candle, and singing Christmas carols. After one song, one of Lori's little sisters looked my direction and said, "Somebody is mumbling." My first Advent participation was less than impressive. The Advent time was simple, meaningful, and short enough for Lori's two younger sisters to stay engaged.

Over the years we have kept Advent as a part of our family tradition. We have used an Advent guide that Lori made in a fourth grade Sunday school class. Although a bit worn, the guide has served us well. Our prayer is that this guide will help you start the Advent tradition with your family.

We do have one request. Please don't make Advent a legalistic ritual. That is not the purpose. We do not celebrate Advent "by the letter of the law." During some Christmas seasons, travel has kept us from celebrating the first Sunday of Advent. College interrupted the flow for a few years.

A few times we have covered a couple of Sundays on Christmas Eve when our whole family was together. No matter what . . . we have always had fun.

There have been long discussions over who would light the candles. We have four children, so thankfully there was a candle for each one! Our daughter Lara was born on Christmas Day, so she always gets to light the Christ candle lit on Christmas Eve or Christmas Day. The wax running down the candles has always been a little too intriguing. Blowing the candles out needed special instruction so hot wax was not sent flying. Our singing has started with the carol of the day and sometimes morphed into a medley of every Christmas song we know with many special effects and as much laughter as singing.

Our prayer is that this guide will help you start a celebration of Advent with your family, keep your Christmas focused on Jesus, and create some fun and meaningful spiritual memories.

May God bless you as you keep your focus on Jesus through this Christmas season and throughout the year.

Ron & Lori Moore

What Is Advent?

Comfort, comfort my people, says your God. Speak tenderly to Jerusalem, and proclaim to her that her hard service has been completed, that her sin has been paid for, that she has received from the LORD's hand double for all her sins. A voice of one calling: "In the wilderness prepare the way for the LORD; make straight in the desert a highway for our God. Every valley shall be raised up, every mountain and hill made low; the rough ground shall become level, the rugged places a plain. And the glory of the LORD will be revealed, and all people will see it together. For the mouth of the LORD has spoken."
—Isaiah 40:1–5

Advent is a Latin word meaning "the coming." Church leaders officially established Advent in the sixth century as a time for Christians to reflect on the true meaning of Christmas.

Advent is celebrated the four Sundays before Christmas in order to help us prepare for the observance of Christmas.

Advent is purposed to be a time of personal reflection and spiritual growth.

The celebration of Advent is a great time for family worship. The weekly celebration helps parents keep focused during the busy Christmas season. When parents are focused, families are focused on the true meaning and purpose of Christ's coming. On a personal note, Advent helped our family establish a time to become familiar with the prophecies and stories surrounding the birth of Jesus. It also helped our children learn the verses of well-known Christmas carols.

The Wreath and the Candles

"You are the light of the world. A town built on a hill cannot be hidden. Neither do people light a lamp and put it under a bowl. Instead they put it on its stand, and it gives light to everyone in the house. In the same way, let your light shine before others, that they may see your good deeds and glorify your Father in heaven."
—Matthew 5:14–16

The wreath and candles provide tangible symbols that help children (and adults) learn and remember key aspects regarding the coming of Jesus. Each candle also reminds us that Jesus is the Light of the world.

While the candles can represent different aspects of Christmas, we have chosen to focus on God's preparation for Christmas with the following themes.

FIRST SUNDAY OF ADVENT:
God Preparing Our Hearts

SECOND SUNDAY OF ADVENT:
God Preparing the World

THIRD SUNDAY OF ADVENT:
God Preparing His Servants

FOURTH SUNDAY OF ADVENT:
God Preparing His Son

CHRISTMAS OR CHRISTMAS EVE:
The Arrival of Jesus!

WEEK 1

FIRST SUNDAY OF ADVENT

God Preparing Our Hearts

KEY IDEA:
Ask God to prepare your heart for Christmas.

KEY VERSE:
"You will seek me and find me when you seek me with all your heart."
—**Jeremiah 29:13 NIV**

CANDLE LIGHTING

As the first candle is lighted, say, "I light this candle on the first Sunday of Advent to remind us that we must prepare ourselves for the coming of Jesus."

WEEK 1

PASSAGE TO READ ALOUD

Come, let us sing for joy to the LORD; let us shout aloud to the Rock of our salvation. Let us come before him with thanksgiving and extol him with music and song. For the LORD is the great God, the great King above all gods. In his hand are the depths of the earth, and the mountain peaks belong to him. The sea is his, for he made it, and his hands formed the dry land. Come, let us bow down in worship, let us kneel before the LORD our Maker; for he is our God and we are the people of his pasture, the flock under his care. **—Psalm 95:1–7 NIV**

O COME, O COME, EMMANUEL

O come, O come, Emmanuel,
And ransom captive Israel,
That mourns in lonely exile here
Until the Son of God appear.

Rejoice! Rejoice! Emmanuel
Shall come to thee, O Israel.

O come, Thou Rod of Jesse, free
Thine own from Satan's tyranny;
From depths of hell Thy people save,
And give them vict'ry o'er the grave.

Rejoice! Rejoice! Emmanuel
Shall come to thee, O Israel.

O come, Thou Day-spring, come and cheer
Our spirits by Thine advent here;
O drive away the shades of night
And pierce the clouds and bring us light.

Rejoice! Rejoice! Emmanuel
Shall come to thee, O Israel.

O come, Thou Key of David, come
And open wide our heavenly home
Where all thy saints with Thee shall dwell—
O come, O come, Emmanuel!

Rejoice! Rejoice! Emmanuel
Shall come to thee, O Israel.

WEEK 1

WEEK 1

O COME, ALL YE FAITHFUL

O come, all ye faithful,
Joyful and triumphant,
Come ye, O come ye to Bethlehem;
Come and behold Him,
Born the King of angels:

O come, let us adore Him, O come, let us adore Him,
O come, let us adore Him, Christ, the Lord.

Sing, choirs of angels,
Sing in exultation,
Sing all ye bright hosts of heav'n above;
Glory to God,
All glory in the highest:

O come, let us adore Him, O come, let us adore Him,
O come, let us adore Him, Christ, the Lord.

Yea, Lord, we greet Thee,
Born this happy morning,
Jesus, to Thee be all glory giv'n;
Word of the Father,
Now in flesh appearing:

O come, let us adore Him, O come, let us adore Him,
O come, let us adore Him, Christ, the Lord.

DEVOTIONAL

Have you ever attended a sporting event when your team scored and won the game?
You jumped straight up with your arms extended into the air! You shouted a loud shout! You pumped your fist! You gave high fives to everyone around you! You could not contain your excitement. You expressed your joy with your entire being.

The writer of Psalm 95 invites us to sing with that same kind of enthusiasm. He calls us to shout loud praises to God. He summons us to sing at the top of our lungs. We are to come before God with thanksgiving. Our God is amazing! He is the "great King above all gods." When we sing songs about God we can demonstrate joy with our entire being.

"O Come, All Ye Faithful" is a song that invites God's people to be joyful and triumphant. Jesus has come! The Savior is here! We can sing with great happiness and excitement. When you come to the chorus sing the first "O come, let us adore Him" quietly. Sing the next "O come, let us adore Him" a little louder. Then belt out the last "O come, let us adore Him, Christ, the Lord." To add to that, how about some high fives for everyone in the room!

Closing Prayer

Heavenly Father, on this first Sunday of Advent we thank you for sending your Son into this world. Thank you that Jesus came to die on the cross for our sins. As we look forward to Christmas, please prepare our hearts. Help us to celebrate this season in a way that honors you. In Jesus' name we pray. _Amen_

MONDAY

"Martha, Martha," the Lord answered, "you are worried and upset about many things, but few things are needed—or indeed only one. Mary has chosen what is better, and it will not be taken away from her." **—Luke 10:41–42 NIV**

Christmas is crazy! There are trees to put up and decorate; lights to string; malls to maneuver; gifts to buy; parties to host; parties to attend; Christmas cantatas; food prep; getting the house ready for relatives; wrapping; traveling; managing expectations (sometimes our children's Christmas list is a bit too long). All some people want for Christmas is for it to be over!

Far too many people go to great lengths in preparing everything for Christmas . . . except their hearts. Everybody in our lives gets what he or she wants . . . except God. In our efforts to get everyone the right gift, we miss the great Gift that God has given to us.

This Christmas let's slow things down. Let's keep things simple. Let's not fall into the "Martha Mentality" and be worried and upset about many things when only one thing should be our focus. Let's follow the "Mary Model" and keep our emphasis on Jesus. After all, it is HIS birthday we are celebrating.

Closing Prayer

Father, slow me down. I feel the Christmas adrenaline flowing already. Keep me focused. There are so many things I feel I need to do. Prepare my heart. Help me to follow Mary's example and choose the better things—the things that will continue after this Christmas season is over. In Jesus' name. *Amen*

NOTES

_____

_____

_____

_____

_____

_____

_____

_____

_____

TUESDAY

"You will seek me and find me when you seek me with all your heart."

—Jeremiah 29:13 NIV

God is not hiding from you. He is not yelling "cold" or "hot" as you maneuver the spiritual journey trying to find him. He desires to be found.

He wants to meet with you. He wants to have a conversation—an ongoing conversation—with you that warms your heart and reminds you of his presence. When you seek him you will find him.

Begin each day conversing with God. Thank him for a new day fresh with his grace and mercy. Tell him what's on your heart. Talk through your schedule with him. Tell him about that meeting you dread, the things you fear, your frustrations, and the things that bring anxiety to your heart. Talk to him about the people you love. Share your joys. Tell him the things you yearn for, the things you dream about. Ask him to remind you of his constant presence throughout the day.

Tell God you want to do Christmas his way this year. Ask him to do his work of preparation in your heart. Ask him to help you lead your family through the season (and beyond) in a way that honors him and serves others. Here's the promise of preparation: When you seek him you will find him when you seek him with all your heart.

Closing Prayer

Father, help me to desire you. I have so many things to do. Help me slow down. Capture my focus and make it yours. Prepare my heart for Christmas. In Jesus' name. *Amen*

NOTES

_____

_____

_____

_____

_____

_____

_____

_____

_____

_____

WEDNESDAY

Come, let us bow down in worship, let us kneel before the LORD our Maker; for he is our God and we are the people of his pasture, the flock under his care.

—Psalm 95:6–7 NIV

Lori always has our children design the menu for the holiday and birthday meals. That way they all get to eat their favorite food. One thing that makes the menu every time is strawberry pretzel salad, and it takes a lot of preparation. First you have to put pretzels in a baggie and beat them to powder (that's the part I like doing). Then you mix the pretzel powder with butter and pack it into a pan. A mixture of cream cheese and cool whip is spread over the pretzels. Then strawberry Jell-O is poured on top. I'm leaving out several steps but you get the idea. This is just one of the regular dishes we make that takes a lot of preparation. In the same way, it takes a lot to prepare our hearts for Christmas.

The psalmist calls for us to bow down and kneel before God. On our knees is not only a posture of reverence, it's a posture of stillness. Driving, walking, and running all describe actions of motion, but kneeling shows that I have reached my destination—God's presence.

Slow down and kneel down. Take time for personal worship. Tell God how much you love him. Tell him that this day belongs to him. Tell him that above all else you desire to honor him today in your thoughts, words, and actions. It is the critical ingredient in heart preparation.

I know that you are busy—too busy not to kneel down and worship.

Closing Prayer

Father, my calendar is full today. Most of my day I will be running, but right now I kneel and bow before you. I acknowledge you as the Maker of heaven and earth and as my Abba, Father. I desire to live today under your guidance and care. In Jesus' name. *Amen*

NOTES

_____

_____

_____

_____

_____

_____

_____

_____

_____

THURSDAY

"But seek first his kingdom and his righteousness, and all these things will be given to you as well." —Matthew 6:33 NIV

Do you spend most of your time focusing on "these things"? The right career. The right home. The right school for your kids. The right activities for the kids. The right retirement plan. The right getaways. Especially during this time of year, all the right gifts for those you love. "These things" are not bad things. In fact, Jesus says that he will give you all the things you need, as long as you focus on first things first.

The kingdom order starts with preparing our hearts. Busyness with secondary things keeps us from focusing on the primary thing. However, giving attention to first things first allows all the other things in our lives to fall into their proper places and times.

The kingdom order prepares our hearts. It helps us keep our focus (and our family's focus) on God and what he wants our Christmas (and our lives) to be. When we seek first things first, he promises to take care of the rest.

Closing Prayer

Father, as I seek you first today, give me the needed confirmation that you really will take care of the other things in my life. In Jesus' name. *Amen*

NOTES

_____

_____

_____

_____

_____

_____

_____

_____

_____

_____

_____

FRIDAY

Be kind and compassionate to one another, forgiving each other, just as in Christ God forgave you. —Ephesians 4:32 NIV

C. S. Lewis said that forgiveness is a "lovely idea" until you actually have to do it. True, isn't it? We love the biblical principle. We're not so convinced about the practical application. However, forgiveness is a major part of heart preparation.

The Christmas season takes our emotions on a roller coaster ride. The parent who left will want us to stop by. The sibling we haven't talked to all year will be at the family Christmas get-together. We have to buy a gift for the relative whose reckless words still sting. No family is perfect and imperfections are highlighted during Christmas.

As you ask God to prepare your heart this Christmas, it's time for some practical application. Who do you need to forgive? Make a phone call, write a letter, send an email or have that personal conversation. Forgive others, "just as in Christ God forgave you." I don't know what the response of the other person will be. I just know that living without forgiveness is an emotional prison. Forgiveness sets the prisoner free.

Closing Prayer

Father, I know that my heart cannot be prepared for Christmas if I don't follow the instruction of your Word. Help me forgive others just as in Christ you have forgiven me. Don't let me get hung up on the response of others to my call, email, letter, or personal conversation. Help me to forgive and move forward in freedom. In Jesus' name. *Amen*

NOTES

_____

_____

_____

_____

_____

_____

_____

_____

_____

SATURDAY

"You are the salt of the earth. But if the salt loses its saltiness, how can it be made salty again? It is no longer good for anything, except to be thrown out and trampled underfoot. You are the light of the world. A town built on a hill cannot be hidden."

—Matthew 5:13–14 NIV

Salt is unlike anything else. It changes the taste of everything it is mixed with. When something comes into contact with salt, it is changed. Light is unlike anything else. Light cannot not be light (sorry for the double negative). Its property displays its existence.

Jesus said that you, believer, are salt and light! As a new creation you make an impact on the people around you. As a follower of Jesus your life cuts through the spiritual darkness and illuminates the path to God. This Christmas you can demonstrate to family and friends what you believe in and what you stand for. With a heart prepared for impact you can create change and dispel the darkness around you.

Dietrich Bonhoeffer said it this way: "Since you are that light, you can no longer remain hidden, even if you want to. It is the property of light to shine. A city set on a hill cannot be hid; it can be seen for miles away." You are the salt of the earth! You are the light of the world! This Christmas season it is time for you to shine!

Closing Prayer

Father, prepare our hearts for impact! Prepare us to shine! Use us this Christmas to bring family and friends into a relationship with you through your Son, Jesus Christ. In his name we pray. *Amen*

NOTES

_____

_____

_____

_____

_____

_____

_____

_____

_____

_____

_____

WEEK 2

SECOND SUNDAY OF ADVENT

God Preparing the World

KEY IDEA:
God prepared the world for the coming of his Son.

KEY VERSE:
"But you, Bethlehem Ephrathah, though you are small among the clans of Judah, out of you will come for me one who will be ruler over Israel, whose origins are from of old, from ancient times."
—Micah 5:2 NIV

CANDLE LIGHTING

As you light the candle for the first Sunday say, "On the first Sunday of Advent we began to prepare our hearts for the first coming of Jesus. Now with prepared hearts, let's see how God prepared the world."

As the second candle is lighted, say, "I light this candle on the second Sunday of Advent to remind us that God prepared the world for the coming of Jesus."

WEEK 2

PASSAGE TO READ ALOUD

For to us a child is born, to us a son is given, and the government will be on his shoulders. And he will be called Wonderful Counselor, Mighty God, Everlasting Father, Prince of Peace. Of the greatness of his government and peace there will be no end. He will reign on David's throne and over his kingdom, establishing and upholding it with justice and righteousness from that time on and forever. The zeal of the LORD Almighty will accomplish this. **—Isaiah 9:6–7 NIV**

O LITTLE TOWN OF BETHLEHEM

O little town of Bethlehem, how still we see thee lie!
Above thy deep and dreamless sleep
The silent stars go by;
Yet in thy dark streets shineth
The everlasting Light—
The hopes and fears of all the years
Are met in thee tonight.

For Christ is born of Mary—and gathered all above,
While mortals sleep, the angels keep
Their watch of wond'ring love.
O morning stars, together
Proclaim the holy birth,
And praises sing to God the King,
And peace to men on earth.

How silently, how silently, the wondrous gift is giv'n!
So God imparts to human hearts
The blessings of His heav'n.
No ear may hear His coming,
But, in this world of sin,
Where meek souls will receive Him still
The dear Christ enters in.

O holy Child of Bethlehem, descend to us, we pray;
Cast out our sin and enter in—
Be born in us today.
We hear the Christmas angels
The great glad tidings tell;
O come to us, abide with us,
Our Lord Emmanuel!

WEEK 2

IT CAME UPON THE MIDNIGHT CLEAR

It came upon the midnight clear,
That glorious song of old,
From angels bending near the earth
To touch their harps of gold:
"Peace on the earth, goodwill to men,
From heav'n's all gracious King!"
The world in solemn stillness lay
To hear the angels sing.

And ye, beneath life's crushing load,
Whose forms are bending low,
Who toil along the climbing way
With painful steps and slow,
Look now! for glad and golden hours
Come swiftly on the wing:
O rest beside the weary road
And hear the angels sing.

DEVOTIONAL

Jesus is the Wonderful Counselor. I can go to him anytime for anything. He is never too busy. No appointment needed. He understands. He sympathizes with my weaknesses. He was tempted in every way that I am, yet he never gave in. His perfect counsel corrects my self-counsel and selfish thinking. The Wonderful Counselor gives guidance to my foolish heart.

Jesus is the Mighty God. All things were created by and for him. Apart from him nothing was made that has been made. He touched blind eyes and they saw. He touched withered limbs and they were normal and healthy. He calmed the raging storm. He raised the dead. He arose from the dead and destroyed the last enemy.

Jesus is the Everlasting Father. From everlasting to everlasting he is God. The Word became flesh in the manger, but there has never been a time when Jesus was not nor will there ever be a time when he is not.

Jesus is the Prince of Peace. He reigns as King and one day will bring eternal peace to the earth, but now he brings peace to the heart. He said, "Peace I leave with you; my peace I give you. I do not give to you as the world gives. Do not let your hearts be troubled and do not be afraid," (John 14:27).

For unto us a child is born! Enter the King! Exit the darkness! The Light of the world has come!

Closing Prayer

Heavenly Father, thank you for preparing the world for Jesus. Thank you for letting us see the prophesies given and fulfilled. Thank you for loving the world so much that you sent your only Son to do for us what we could never do for ourselves. In his name we pray. *Amen*

MONDAY

"But you, Bethlehem Ephrathah, though you are small among the clans of Judah, out of you will come for me one who will be ruler over Israel, whose origins are from of old, from ancient times. . . . And he will be our peace." —Micah 5:2, 4–5a NIV

Seven hundred years before the birth of Jesus, the prophet Micah told about his coming. Micah told where Jesus would be born and the clan from which he would come. Micah explained that the One coming was eternal; his beginning was before his birth. The Messiah would shepherd his people and lead them with strength. The Coming One "will be our peace."

Man cannot stand before the righteous God. Our sin separates us from him. There exists a great chasm between the holy God and sinful man, but Jesus came to change all that.

He came to bridge the gap. By his payment for our sins on the cross Jesus provided the way for us to have peace with God.

Do you have that peace? Have you trusted in Christ as the only way that you can know God and enter into a relationship with him? Are you certain that you will be at peace with God for eternity? If not, I invite you to pray this prayer.

Closing Prayer

Dear God, I know that I am a sinner and am separated from you because of my sin. I know that I cannot earn my way to you or somehow make myself good enough for you. I know that I do not have peace with you, but I want to. Right now I trust in Jesus as the only way that I can have the peace that I long for. I trust in Jesus as the only way I can have a relationship with you. I am sorry for my sins. I long for your forgiveness. Thank you for the promise that through Jesus I can have peace with you. In his name I pray. *Amen*

NOTES

_____

_____

_____

_____

_____

_____

_____

_____

_____

TUESDAY

"Therefore the Lord himself will give you a sign: The virgin will conceive and give birth to a son, and will call him Immanuel." —Isaiah 7:14 NIV

Matthew 1:23 . . . they will call him Immanuel (which means "God with us").

His name is *Immanuel* . . . even when the doctor says, "It's cancer."
His name is *Immanuel* . . . even in the darkest night.
His name is *Immanuel* . . . even when she says, "I don't love you anymore."
His name is *Immanuel* . . . even when he walks out the door.
His name is *Immanuel* . . . even when your heart is breaking.
His name is *Immanuel* . . . even as you walk away from the grave.
His name is Immanuel . . . even in the midst of grief.
His name is *Immanuel* . . . even when you feel alone.
His name is *Immanuel* . . . even when the job goes away.
His name is *Immanuel* . . . even when your child won't come home.

His name is and will always be *Immanuel*.

"The LORD your God is with you, the Mighty Warrior who saves. He will take great delight in you; in his love he will no longer rebuke you, but will rejoice over you with singing" (Zephaniah 3:17).

Closing Prayer

Lord Jesus, thank you for always being with us. Thank you for the promise that you will never leave us. Thank you for being Immanuel! *Amen*

NOTES

_____

_____

_____

_____

_____

_____

_____

_____

_____

WEDNESDAY

"Remember the former things, those of long ago; I am God, and there is no other; I am God, and there is none like me . . . 'My purpose will stand, and I will do all that I please."

—Isaiah 46:9–10 NIV

Regardless of the economic forecast *. . . I am God and there is no other . . . My purpose will stand.* Regardless of legislative decisions *. . . I am God and there is no other . . . My purpose will stand.* Regardless of who sits in the Oval Office *. . . I am God and there is no other . . . My purpose will stand.* Regardless of the international turmoil *. . . I am God and there is no other . . . My purpose will stand.* Regardless of the rogue rulers who make great claims *. . . I am God and there is no other . . . My purpose will stand.*

Even when the doctor's report was not what I wanted to hear . . . even when he walks away . . . even when my heart is broken . . . even when I wait for God to answer . . . even when my dream dies . . . even when I don't get the job . . . even when my child is estranged . . . even when I am discouraged . . . even when I am depressed . . . even when I don't feel like pushing forward . . . even when grief hits me like a vicious upper cut . . . even when things don't make sense . . . REMEMBER—*I am God and there is no other . . . My purpose will stand.*

Closing Prayer

Father, wherever we stand today . . . whether it is in joy, sadness, disappointment, discouragement, confusion, fear, impatience, or anxiety . . . we proclaim that you are God and there is no other. We thank you that your purpose will always stand. In Jesus' name. *Amen*

NOTES

_____

_____

_____

_____

_____

_____

_____

_____

_____

THURSDAY

But he was pierced for our transgressions, he was crushed for our iniquities; the punishment that brought us peace was on him, and by his wounds we are healed.

—Isaiah 53:5 NIV

Jesus was given no advantages. The Father sent him to the back of the line and made him experience all the pain of humanity. He was not strikingly handsome or a head taller than the rest of the crowd—*He had no beauty or majesty to attract us to him . . .* He was not accepted by society—*He was despised and rejected by mankind . . .* Although fully God, he was not born with a silver spoon in his mouth—*a man of suffering, and familiar with pain.*

Jesus came from heaven to earth and was sent to the back of the line—stricken, smitten, afflicted, pierced, crushed, oppressed, a lamb to the slaughter, cut off from the land of the living. The King of Kings lived life as the king of suffering. He was not a victim of circumstance. He was not in the wrong place at the wrong time. He was sent to the back of the line by the Father—it was the Lord's will to crush him and cause him to suffer.

Jesus was given no advantages in life and died a brutal death. That's what it took to pay the penalty of sin. Nothing less would do. Jesus left heaven and went to the back of the line for you and me. I was the one who went astray. I was the one who turned to my own way. God laid my sin on Jesus. There is only one way to respond to such love—fall down and worship him! Every day! With your whole life!

Closing Prayer

Lord Jesus, thank you for willingly going to the back of the line for me. *Amen*

NOTES

_____

_____

_____

_____

_____

_____

_____

_____

_____

_____

FRIDAY

Rejoice greatly, Daughter Zion! Shout, Daughter Jerusalem! See, your king comes to you, righteous and victorious, lowly and riding on a donkey, on a colt, the foal of a donkey. —Zechariah 9:9 NIV

Through Zechariah, God prepared the world for Jesus. The prophet explained that the coming king would not show up as an overbearing conqueror. He would gently demonstrate love and compassion. Righteousness would characterize his person and his reign. It was the custom of the day for a king coming for battle to ride on a war stallion. One coming in peace rode on a donkey.

Five hundred years after Zechariah's prophecy, Jesus rode into Jerusalem on a donkey. Many welcomed him by shouting, "Hosanna to the Son of David!" "Blessed is he who comes in the name of the Lord!" "Hosanna in the highest!" The large crowd spread their cloaks out on the road. Others cut branches from trees and spread them before Jesus, but by the end of that week the fickle crowd was shouting, "Crucify him!"

The people wanted a powerful king to deliver them from the rule of Rome. Jesus came as a servant to deliver them from the rule of sin. They wanted a king to reign. Jesus came to die. They wanted a national revolt. Jesus came to bring spiritual peace between a holy God and sinful man. In the busyness of this Christmas season, slow down and thank God that Jesus is our peace.

Closing Prayer

Lord Jesus, my Christmas has become about lists. Lists of things I want, need to buy, and need to do. My prayers are often about lists as well. Like the people who greeted you as you rode into Jerusalem, I want you to do certain things for me. Help me to desire your peace instead of presents and possessions. In your name I pray. *Amen*

NOTES

_____

_____

_____

_____

_____

_____

_____

_____

_____

SATURDAY

"Come now, let us settle the matter," says the LORD. "Though your sins are like scarlet, they shall be as white as snow; though they are red as crimson, they shall be like wool."
—Isaiah 1:18 NIV

God wants to give you a great gift this Christmas. He wants to give you the great gift of forgiveness all wrapped up in the work of Jesus. Our sins cause us to fall short of God's holy standard. Baptism, confirmation, generous giving, regular church attendance, and good works are not enough to make us right with God. We are in a helpless and hopeless situation, so God sent Jesus to do for us what we could not do for ourselves.

Jesus purchased God's great gift of forgiveness by his death on the cross. He alone paid the penalty for our sins. Accepting the free gift is simply this: Believing that Jesus died for me. Believing that the death of Jesus paid the penalty for my sins. Trusting in Jesus alone to place me into an eternal relationship with the living God. My sins are as red as crimson. Through the work of Jesus, they are made as white as fresh snow and pure white wool.

God wants to settle the matter with you. God loves you and desires to know you intimately and deeply. Today I urge you to trust in Jesus as the only way the stain of your sin can be washed away and forgiven. The following prayer is a guide to help you settle the matter with God.

Closing Prayer

Heavenly Father, I know that I am a sinner and cannot earn my way to you. My best efforts on my best day fall short. Right now I trust in Jesus alone as the only way I can have a relationship with you. I trust in Jesus as the one who paid the penalty of sin by his death on the cross, one-time-for-all-time. Thank you for hearing my prayer, forgiving my sins, and placing me in your family. In Jesus' name. *Amen*

NOTES

WEEK 3

THIRD SUNDAY OF ADVENT

God Preparing His Servants

KEY IDEA:
God prepared his servants to announce the arrival of Jesus.

KEY VERSE:
While they were there, the time came for the baby to be born, and she gave birth to her firstborn, a son. She wrapped him in cloths and placed him in a manger, because there was no guest room available for them.
—Luke 2:6–7 NIV

CANDLE LIGHTING

As you light the first two candles say, "On the first Sunday of Advent we asked God to prepare our hearts to focus on Jesus during this Christmas season. On the second Sunday of Advent we saw how God prepared the world for the coming of his Son. Today we are going to see how God prepared his servants to announce the arrival of Jesus."

As the third candle is lighted, say, "I light this candle on the third Sunday of Advent to remind us that God prepared his people for the arrival of Jesus."

WEEK 3

PASSAGE TO READ ALOUD

And there were shepherds living out in the fields nearby, keeping watch over their flocks at night. An angel of the Lord appeared to them, and the glory of the Lord shone around them, and they were terrified. But the angel said to them, "Do not be afraid. I bring you good news that will cause great joy for all the people. Today in the town of David a Savior has been born to you; he is the Messiah, the Lord. This will be a sign to you: You will find a baby wrapped in cloths and lying in a manger."

Suddenly a great company of the heavenly host appeared with the angel, praising God and saying, "Glory to God in the highest heaven, and on earth peace to those on whom his favor rests."

When the angels had left them and gone into heaven, the shepherds said to one another, "Let's go to Bethlehem and see this thing that has happened, which the Lord has told us about."

So they hurried off and found Mary and Joseph, and the baby, who was lying in the manger. —**Luke 2:8–16 NIV**

HARK! THE HERALD ANGELS SING

Hark! the herald angels sing,
"Glory to the newborn King;
Peace on earth, and mercy mild—
God and sinners reconciled!"
Joyful, all ye nations, rise,
Join the triumph of the skies;
With th'angelic hosts proclaim,
"Christ is born in Bethlehem."
Hark! the herald angels sing,
"Glory to the newborn King!"

Christ, by highest heav'n adored,
Christ, the everlasting Lord:
Late in time behold Him come,
Offspring of a virgin's womb.
Veiled in flesh the Godhead see,
Hail th'incarnate Deity!
Pleased as man with men to dwell,
Jesus, our Emmanuel.
Hark! the herald angels sing,
"Glory to the newborn King!"

Hail the heav'n born Prince of Peace!
Hail the Sun of Righteousness!
Light and life to all He brings,
Ris'n with healing in His wings.
Mild he lays His glory by,
Born that man no more may die;
Born to raise the sons of earth,
Born to give them second birth.
Hark! the herald angels sing,
"Glory to the newborn King!"

WEEK 3

ANGELS WE HAVE HEARD ON HIGH

Angels we have heard on high,
Sweetly singing o'er the plains,
And the mountains, in reply,
Echoing their joyous strains
Gloria
In excelsis Deo! Gloria
In excelsis Deo!

Shepherds, why this jubilee?
Why your joyous strains prolong?
What the gladsome tidings be
Which inspire your heav'nly song?
Gloria
In excelsis Deo! Gloria
In excelsis Deo!

Come to Bethlehem and see
Him whose birth the angels sing;
Come, adore on bended knee
Christ the Lord, the newborn King.
Gloria
In excelsis Deo! Gloria
In excelsis Deo!

DEVOTIONAL

Can you even imagine the emotion of the shepherds? There in the darkness and quietness of night the sky burst into light. The stillness was overtaken by the loud praise of the heavenly host. It's no wonder the shepherds were terrified.

Then the angel addressed the shepherds' fear. The appearance was about "good news that will cause great joy." Jesus had been born! The Messiah had arrived! God had come . . . in the form of a baby wrapped in cloths and lying in a manger. The shepherds hurried off to find the baby, and when they saw Jesus they spread the word.

We often miss the fact that Jesus' entry into our lives is just as dramatic as the angel's announcement to the shepherds.

Our eyes, blinded by sin, are opened. The darkness becomes light. The Spirit brings our deadened heart to life. We turn from our journey away from Christ and begin walking with him. Our eternal destination is changed. God takes up residence in us. That's good news filled with great joy! Let's tell others what Jesus has done for us and what he can do for them. Let's spread the word.

Closing Prayer

Heavenly Father, thank you for preparing your servants to bring Jesus into the world and introduce him as the long-awaited Messiah. Give us the courage to introduce Jesus to our family and friends during this Christmas season. In his name we pray. *Amen*

MONDAY

"'I am the Lord's servant,' Mary answered. 'May your word to me be fulfilled.' Then the angel left her." —Luke 1:38 NIV

Mary spoke these words the day God sent the angel Gabriel to Nazareth. This was Mary's surrender, but not her first thought. Following the angel's greeting, Mary "was greatly troubled at his words." Then the angel delivered the unbelievable news. Mary was going to have a baby. "How will this be," Mary questioned, "since I am a virgin?" Gabriel's explanation was as mysterious as his presence, but his last words nailed the reality of the situation: "For nothing is impossible with God."

"I am the Lord's servant," is Mary's statement of surrender. She was the first person to accept Jesus on his terms. Her engagement with Joseph, the man she loved, would be in jeopardy. Those closest to her would not understand her pregnancy. The small town would be filled with rumors. Despite this, she trusted God and surrendered to his plan.

Many believe that they can draw up the terms of their relationship with Jesus, but that's not how it works with the Lord. Everyone who truly wants to follow hard after Jesus must come to a place of surrender. Like Mary, we must say, "Lord, I am your servant. Use me as your instrument in any way you desire."

Closing Prayer

Lord Jesus, we confess that the place of surrender is difficult, but we desire to be your servants. We surrender ourselves to you. Use us to carry out your plan in our lives. In your name. Amen

NOTES

_____

_____

_____

_____

_____

_____

_____

_____

_____

TUESDAY

When Joseph woke up, he did what the angel of the Lord had commanded him and took Mary home as his wife. —Matthew 1:24 NIV

Today an engagement can be ended simply by returning the ring. For Mary and Joseph, however, the premarital pledge was binding and could be broken only by divorce. Having discovered that Mary was pregnant, Joseph "had in mind to divorce her quietly." That's when an angel came to convince him otherwise. She had not been unfaithful, the angel explained. Her child was "from the Holy Spirit." The son would be named Jesus. He would "save his people from their sins."

The Virgin Birth is an essential doctrine. Jesus was fully man, fully God. As man, he lost none of his deity. As God, he lost none of his humanness. He had to be God to become the sinless sacrifice. He had to be man to die in our place. Two thousand years later, I type those truths so matter-of-factly, but Joseph had to accept it all by faith.

Certainly God did not choose just any woman to be the mother of his Son. Nor did he choose just any man to be his earthly father and mentor. Joseph was a "righteous man" of great faith. Without a modicum of tangible evidence, he accepted God's Word spoken through the angel and took Mary home as his wife. Imagine the ridicule. Imagine the sneers. Imagine the judgment. Imagine the faith of Joseph! God prepared his servant. He still does.

Closing Prayer

Father, may we learn from the obedience of Joseph. We don't have an angel delivering your message, but we have your Word. May we obey it with the radical faith of Joseph. In Jesus' name. *Amen*

NOTES

_____

_____

_____

_____

_____

_____

_____

_____

_____

WEDNESDAY

. . . Magi from the east came to Jerusalem and asked, "Where is the one who has been born king of the Jews?" —Matthew 2:1–2 NIV

On the Christmas cards it's all picture-perfect. With a star illuminating the manger three wise men bow down before the baby Jesus with their camels parked outside; and, of course, at the bottom of the card are the Hallmark words: Wise men still seek him today. However, let's see what Scripture says about these visitors.

What or who is a Magi? These men were magicians or astrologers known for their wisdom. They may have been from Persia. If that is the case, they had knowledge of Scripture that could be traced back to the time of Daniel (see Daniel 5:11).

How many Magi traveled to see Jesus? We don't know for sure. Based on the number of gifts that were presented to Jesus many conclude that there were three. Some traditions even have names for these men, but neither their names nor their number are given in Scripture.

What star did they see? The star that guided them could have been a supernova or a conjunction of planets. One writer says that it was a supernatural reality similar to the Shekinah that led the Israelites in the days of Moses. All we know for sure is that the star was a true miracle of God.

While there are things we don't know about the wise men, here are the things we know for certain. These men made a great sacrifice to see Jesus. They traveled a great distance. They brought their best to him. They sought Jesus and didn't stop until they found him. They worshipped him. That's the heart of the Magi story, and that should be the heart of our Christmas story as well.

Closing Prayer

Father, your Word says that if we seek you we will find you if we seek you with all our hearts. May we, like the magi, truly seek after you. May we truly worship Jesus, our Savior and Lord. In his name we pray. *Amen*

NOTES

_____

_____

_____

_____

_____

_____

_____

_____

_____

_____

THURSDAY

But the angel said to them, "Do not be afraid. I bring you good news that will cause great joy for all the people." —Luke 2:10 NIV

They were minding their sheep and minding their business when the angel suddenly appeared. In an instant the darkness of night turned to brilliant light. The angel, coming from the presence of God, brought with him God's glory and the place lit up! No wonder the shepherds were terrified, but the angel addressed their fears.

Do not be afraid. Those are exactly the words you want to hear when an angel shows up unexpectedly.

I bring you good news . . . The good news was about a Savior. The long-expected Messiah had arrived. Nothing would ever be the same again.

. . . that will cause great joy . . . The arrival of the Messiah was the arrival of true peace. Through the work of Jesus sinful man could be united with the holy God. A person bound for hell could have the free gift of eternal life. That is the cause of unspeakable joy!

. . . for all the people. The arrival of the Messiah was not for a select few. God's free gift was for all people. God so loved the world that he gave his one and only Son. Whoever trusts in Jesus as the only way to have a relationship with the living God is given eternal life.

God's great gift is for all people. My challenge to you this Christmas is to share it with a few. Share it with your neighbor across the street, the people in your office, and the people you interact with on a daily basis. Let them know that fear can be chased away by the peace that comes through Jesus. Announce to those in your world the Good News that will cause great joy.

Closing Prayer

Father, thank you for bringing someone into my life that shared the Good News with me. This Christmas season help me to share that same Good News with those you have placed in my life. In Jesus' name. *Amen*

NOTES

_____

_____

_____

_____

_____

_____

_____

_____

_____

FRIDAY

"This child is destined to cause the falling and rising of many in Israel, and to be a sign that will be spoken against, so that the thoughts of many hearts will be revealed."

—Luke 2:34–35 NIV

After the birth of Jesus, Mary had to wait forty days before going to the temple to offer a sacrifice for her purification. Mary and Joseph's sacrifice of birds instead of a lamb shows that Jesus was born into a poor family (Luke 2:24). From Mary's "scandalous" pregnancy, to a birth in the place where animals were kept, to an upbringing in a poor family, the Father stripped every royal privilege from his Son.

At the temple there was a "righteous and devout" man named Simeon. He was waiting for the coming Messiah. When Simeon saw Jesus, he took the baby in his arms and broke out in praise. Simeon called Jesus "a light for revelation to the Gentiles and for the glory to your people Israel." He noted that Jesus would cause the rising and falling of many in Israel. As the only way to God, many would believe and be saved; and many would reject Jesus and be separated from God forever.

Then Simeon added a hard truth. He told Mary, "And a sword will pierce your own soul too." With the baby Jesus only forty days old, Simeon prepared Mary for her newborn's sufferings and death. Mary, too, would suffer as she watched Jesus go through the pain of rejection and the agony of the cross. The reminder of suffering surrounded Jesus from the first days of his life.

Closing Prayer

Father, as we celebrate Christmas don't let us forget the mission of Jesus. You sent your Son to pay for the penalty of my sins. Don't let me get so busy with presents that I miss your purpose for Christmas. In Jesus' name. *Amen*

NOTES

_____

_____

_____

_____

_____

_____

_____

_____

_____

_____

SATURDAY

In those days John the Baptist came, preaching in the wilderness of Judea and saying, "Repent, for the kingdom of heaven has come." . . . People went out to him from Jerusalem and all Judea and the whole region of the Jordan. Confessing their sins, they were baptized by him in the Jordan River. —Matthew 3:1–2, 5–6 NIV

John the Baptist made his days count. He lived life plain and simple—camel hair clothes and a leather belt; roasted locusts (surely he didn't eat them raw) and wild honey to eat. What impresses me most, though, is that John the Baptist was a man who knew his purpose. He was on Earth to prepare the world for Jesus, and he never wavered. He lived with spiritual focus. Isn't that the kind of life you want to live?

Let's do Christmas differently. Let's follow John's lead and prepare the people around us for Jesus. Tell the people in your world why Jesus came. Explain to them why he died. Show people how Jesus has transformed your life. Let them know how they can have a relationship with the Savior.

Let's make Christmas count. Let's use the opportunities throughout this season to prepare the way for Jesus, and let's keep sharing the Good News throughout the year.

Closing Prayer

Father, remind me often to keep my eyes fixed on Jesus. Remind me to pick up the pace and follow hard after him. Remind me when I need to slow down and regain my focus. Help me to be a preparer of the way. For Christ's sake. *Amen*

NOTES

WEEK 4

FOURTH SUNDAY OF ADVENT

God Preparing His Son

KEY IDEA:
God prepared his Son to be a sacrifice for us.

KEY VERSE:
He went to Nazareth, where he had been brought up, and on the Sabbath day he went into the synagogue, as was his custom. He stood up to read, and the scroll of the prophet Isaiah was handed to him. . . . The eyes of everyone in the synagogue were fastened on him. He began by saying to them, "Today this scripture is fulfilled in your hearing." **—Luke 4:16–21 NIV**

CANDLE LIGHTING

As you light the previous candles say, "The first Sunday of Advent we asked God to prepare our hearts for Christmas. On the second Sunday of Advent we saw how God prepared the world. On the third Sunday of Advent we considered how God prepared his servants to bring Jesus into the world. Today let's focus on God's great love. He loved us so much that he sent his only Son to pay the penalty for our sins on the cross."

As the fourth candle is lighted, say, "I light this candle on the fourth Sunday of Advent to remind us that God prepared his Son to save his people from their sins."

WEEK 4

PASSAGE TO READ ALOUD

In the beginning was the Word, and the Word was with God, and the Word was God. He was with God in the beginning. Through him all things were made; without him nothing was made that has been made. In him was life, and that life was the light of all mankind. The light shines in the darkness, and the darkness has not overcome it. . . .

The true light that gives light to everyone was coming into the world. He was in the world, and though the world was made through him, the world did not recognize him. He came to that which was his own, but his own did not receive him. Yet to all who did receive him, to those who believed in his name, he gave the right to become children of God—children born not of natural descent, nor of human decision or a husband's will, but born of God. The Word became flesh and made his dwelling among us. We have seen his glory, the glory of the one and only Son, who came from the Father, full of grace and truth.

(John testified concerning him. He cried out, saying, "This is the one I spoke about when I said, 'He who comes after me has surpassed me because he was before me.'") Out of his fullness we have all received grace in place of grace already given. For the law was given through Moses; grace and truth came through Jesus Christ. No one has ever seen God, but the one and only Son, who is himself God and is in closest relationship with the Father, has made him known. **—John 1:1–5, 9–18 NIV**

AWAY IN A MANGER

Away in a manger,
No crib for a bed,
The little Lord Jesus laid down His sweet head;
The stars in the sky
Looked down where He lay,
The little Lord Jesus,
Asleep on the hay.

The cattle are lowing,
The Baby awakes,
But little Lord Jesus, no crying He makes;
I love Thee, Lord Jesus!
Look down from the sky,
And stay by my cradle
Till morning is nigh.

Be near me, Lord Jesus,
I ask Thee to stay
Close by me forever, and love me, I pray;
Bless all the dear children
In Thy tender care,
And fit us for heaven,
To live with Thee there.

WEEK 4

SILENT NIGHT! HOLY NIGHT!

Silent night! holy night!
All is calm, all is bright
Round yon virgin
Mother and Child,
Holy Infant, so tender and mild—
Sleep in heavenly peace,
Sleep in heavenly peace.

Silent night! holy night!
Shepherds quake at the sight;
Glories stream from heaven afar,
Heav'nly hosts sing alleluia—
Christ the Savior is born!
Christ the Savior is born!

Silent night! holy night!
Son of God, love's pure light
Radiant beams from
Thy holy face
With the dawn of redeeming grace—
Jesus, Lord at Thy birth,
Jesus, Lord at Thy birth.

DEVOTIONAL

Tiny hands waving about uncontrollably. A shrill cry piercing the damp air of a borrowed cave. A mother's peaceful smile. A mysterious smile on the face of her husband who helped deliver a miracle. *The Word became flesh: God confined to an infant.*

Growing hands pointing to ancient scrolls. An adolescent voice asking and answering questions. The teachers amazed. A mother who "treasured all these things in her heart." The Father smiling with favor. *The Word became flesh: God growing in stature.*

Gentle hands touching blind eyes, deaf ears, and withered limbs. Powerful hands turning water into wine, feeding multitudes with a single meal, and touching life into lifeless bodies. Thankful faces without words to express their gratitude. *The Word became flesh: The Father glorified through the Son.*

Constricted hands, the result of spikes driven through his wrists. Arms outstretched, fastened to a wooden beam. A mother stands below feeling every painful throb as her own. The just Father turns his back on his Son. *The Word became flesh: Our sins on Jesus.*

Scarred hands in resurrected glory. A chariot of clouds lifting him to the Father. A joyful mother watching her Son ascend. A promise from the lips of the risen Savior: Just as I go, I will return again. *The Word became flesh: Resurrection assurance.*

Open hands inviting every sinner to himself, accepting all who come to him in faith. Blind eyes see. Prison doors are opened. The prince or pauper, none are turned away. Eternal life to all who believe. *The Word became flesh: Sinful man in communion with the holy God!*

Closing Prayer

Heavenly Father, thank you for sending your Son into the world to die for our sins. Thank you that everyone who trusts in Jesus will have eternal life. Give us the courage to share Jesus with our families and friends during this Christmas season. In his name we pray. *Amen*

CHRISTMAS

The Arrival of Jesus!

KEY IDEA:
The arrival of Jesus brought hope to the world.

KEY VERSE:
When Jesus spoke again to the people, he said,
"I am the light of the world. Whoever follows me will never
walk in darkness, but will have the light of life."
—John 8:12 NIV

CANDLE LIGHTING

As you light the previous candles say, "The first Sunday of Advent we asked God to prepare our hearts for Christmas. On the second Sunday of Advent we saw how God prepared the world. On the third Sunday of Advent we considered how God prepared his servants to bring Jesus into the world. On the fourth Sunday of Advent we learned that God loved us so much that he sent Jesus to pay the penalty for our sins on the cross. Today we celebrate Jesus' birthday. The King is born!"

As the Christmas candle is lighted, say, "I light this Christmas candle to remind us that Jesus, the Light of the world, has come."

PASSAGE TO READ ALOUD

In those days Caesar Augustus issued a decree that a census should be taken of the entire Roman world. (This was the first census that took place while Quirinius was governor of Syria.) And everyone went to their own town to register.

So Joseph also went up from the town of Nazareth in Galilee to Judea, to Bethlehem the town of David, because he belonged to the house and line of David. He went there to register with Mary, who was pledged to be married to him and was expecting a child. While they were there, the time came for the baby to be born, and she gave birth to her firstborn, a son. She wrapped him in cloths and placed him in a manger, because there was no guest room available for them. **—Luke 2:1–7 NIV**

THE FIRST NOEL

The first noel the angel did say
Was to certain poor shepherds
In fields as they lay—
In fields where they lay keeping their sheep,
On a cold winter's night that was so deep.

Noel, noel! Noel, noel!
Born is the King of Israel!

They looked up and saw a star
Shining in the east,
Beyond them far;
And to the earth it gave great light,
And so it continued both day and night.

Noel, noel! Noel, noel!
Born is the King of Israel!

Then let us all with one accord
Sing praises
To our heav'nly Lord,
That hath made heav'n and earth of naught,
And with his blood mankind hath bought.

Noel, noel! Noel, noel!
Born is the King of Israel!

JOY TO THE WORLD!

Joy to the world! the Lord is come!
Let earth receive her King;
Let ev'ry heart prepare Him room,
And heav'n and nature sing,
And heav'n and nature sing,
And heav'n and heav'n and nature sing.

Joy to the earth! the Savior reigns!
Let men their songs employ;
While fields and floods, rocks, hills and plains
Repeat the sounding joy,
Repeat the sounding joy,
Repeat, repeat the sounding joy.

No more let sins and sorrows grow
Nor thorns infest the ground;
He comes to make His blessings flow
Far as the curse is found,
Far as the curse is found,
Far as, far as the curse is found.

He rules the world with truth and grace,
And makes the nations prove
The glories of His righteousness,
And wonders of His love,
And wonders of His love,
And wonders, wonders of His love.

DEVOTIONAL

No breaks. The decree could not have come at a worse time. Mary was in the last days of her pregnancy. The 70-mile trip from Nazareth to Bethlehem over rough terrain was challenging to say the least. They arrived just in time.

No room. Joseph and Mary were not the only ones who made the trip to register. The city was swarming with people. Every possible place to sleep was taken. They settled for a barn.

No advantages. Jesus was born in a little village to an unwed mother from a backwoods town and placed in a feeding bin. The word was out that he was an illegitimate child. Not quite the start you'd expect for a king.

God tiptoed quietly into humanity. The Creator in a cradle. The Wonderful Counselor wrapped in cloths. The Mighty God placed in a manger. The Everlasting Father in flesh. The Prince of Peace in a world of sin. Nevertheless, Jesus came as the Lamb of God to take away the sins of the world. On the cross he paid sin's penalty. He bought us back from sin's slavery. He freed us from sin's prison.

Now, here's the question: Have you trusted in Jesus Christ alone as the Lamb of God who paid the penalty for your sins? Have you trusted in Jesus as the only one who can place you into an eternal relationship with God? You can't save yourself. Only Jesus can save you. Trust him completely to take you through this life and one day carry you home.

Closing Prayer

Heavenly Father, thank you for Jesus. Thank you for sending him for us. Help us to celebrate Christmas every day knowing that the greatest gift we can give others is him. In his name we pray. *Amen*

JOURNAL

_____

_____

_____

_____

_____

_____

_____

_____

_____

_____

JOURNAL

_____

_____

_____

_____

_____

_____

_____

_____

_____

JOURNAL

_____

_____

_____

_____

_____

_____

_____

_____

_____

JOURNAL

_____

_____

_____

_____

_____

_____

_____

_____

_____

JOURNAL

_____

_____

_____

_____

_____

_____

_____

_____

_____

JOURNAL

_____

_____

_____

_____

_____

_____

_____

_____

_____

JOURNAL

_____

_____

_____

_____

_____

_____

_____

_____

_____

_____

JOURNAL

_____

_____

_____

_____

_____

_____

_____

_____

_____

_____

JOURNAL

_____

_____

_____

_____

_____

_____

_____

_____

_____

JOURNAL

_____

_____

_____

_____

_____

_____

_____

_____

_____

JOURNAL

_____

_____

_____

_____

_____

_____

_____

_____

_____

Printed in the USA
CPSIA information can be obtained
at www.ICGtesting.com
LVHW080909251123
764666LV00017B/1850

9 781942 464402